THE
UNOFFICIAL
WITCHER
COOKBOOK

THE
UNOFFICIAL
WITCHER
COOKBOOK

DARINGLY DELICIOUS RECIPES FOR FANS OF THE FANTASY CLASSIC

Nevyana Dimitrova
Trey Guillory

ULYSSES PRESS

Published by:
ULYSSES PRESS
PO Box 3440
Berkeley, CA 94703
www.ulyssespress.com

ISBN: 978-1-64604-412-2
Library of Congress Control Number: 2022936265

Printed in China
10 9 8 7 6 5 4 3 2 1

Acquisitions editor: Kierra Sondereker
Managing editor: Claire Chun
Editor: Michele Anderson
Proofreader: Renee Rutledge
Front cover design: David Hastings
Interior design and layout: Winnie Liu
Photographs: Nevyana Dimitrova
Illustrations: from shutterstock.com—page 8 landscape © Kirk Mason; page 9 wolf © Vasya Kobelev; page 10 tavern © IG Digital Arts; recipe swords © 3xy

"A true witcher should never abandon poultry in distress."

—Geralt

CONTENTS

INTRODUCTION

For nearly thirty years, fantasy lovers everywhere have been captivated by the stoic, white-haired witcher Geralt and his adventures with nightmarish monsters, cunning sorceresses, foolish kings, and inescapable destiny.

In the midst of all this new Witcher content we've been blessed with lately—from books and graphic novels to video games and TV shows that originate with Andrzej Sapkowski and his team—now is the perfect time for the rest of us to immerse ourselves in the mysterious and magical world of *The Witcher* by exploring our own culinary creativity.

Enter *The Unofficial Witcher Cookbook.* This cookbook is a celebration of *The Witcher* saga, its characters, and its contribution to the world of epic fantasy as we know it. What better way to celebrate than by cooking up and eating deliciously rustic meals that make you feel as if you could ride through the Continent and defeat monsters yourself?

Your first foray through these pages will get you hooked on the classic dishes found in the small-town taverns and inns that Geralt happened upon in his travels. Enjoy meals like Fisherman's Stew, Peasant Porridge, and simpler yet tasty meals that are sure to fill your belly until you make your way to the next tavern.

Between destinations, you'll also need food for your journey on the road. The next section of this cookbook will have you preparing hearty dishes to help ease your hunger as you travel through forests, over mountains, or even across oceans. From Mountain Meat Pies to Roadside Sweet Rolls, these recipes are perfect for packing in your saddlebags for a long journey or cooking over the campfire on a chilly night spent resting under the stars.

Tired of living the rough-and-ready life of a witcher constantly on the road? The next section of this cookbook will have you settling into a royal court and feasting on the very best dishes kings and queens have to offer. Get a taste of only the finest meats and wines, with dishes like Duck Confit and Spiced Lamb Chops. And who knows? You just might finish the banquet with a full stomach and a child of surprise.

Before you leave the comfort of those royal banquet halls and head out to catch a djinn or battle a ghoul, you have to partake in royal desserts. Only the very best sweets are served in the noble courts of the Continent. Get your fill of dishes like Chocolate Goddess Cake and Honey Cakes for a Coin before you return to your life on the road.

While many of the original ingredients and recipes for these meals stem from the fabled land of the Continent, substitutes can be found in our world and ordinary markets. It may, however, be difficult to cook some of these dishes without chaos magic, but many of our world's ordinary kitchens should suffice.

These fun recipes can give you the sense of adventure you long for in a world far more magical than our own. Best of all, they are perfect for snacks, family meals, dinner parties, celebrations, book club get-togethers as you discuss *The Witcher* saga, or even watch parties as you and your friends enjoy a marathon session of the newest season of *The Witcher.*

Now grab your sword, pack some spices, and get ready to start out on your most daring culinary crusade yet!

TAVERN FARE

BAKED APPLE BREAKFAST

Rarely are witchers met with excitement or gratitude when arriving in a new town. Instead, the white-haired witcher is often met with sneers and threats. It's only when he meets a girl born under an accursed eclipse that he's shown any kindness in sharing her simple apple breakfast.

3 tablespoons unsalted butter, softened

¼ cup brown sugar

½ teaspoon ground cinnamon

⅛ teaspoon ground nutmeg

1 teaspoon vanilla extract

¼ cup rolled oats

2 tablespoons raisins

5 large apples, rinsed and patted dry

¾ cup warm water

1. Preheat the oven to 375°F.

2. Put the butter, sugar, cinnamon, nutmeg, and vanilla in a large bowl, and mash the mixture together with a fork. Add the oats and raisins and stir them into the mixture. Set aside.

3. Using a sharp paring knife, core each apple about ¾ of the way down. Use a small spoon to carefully dig out the core.

4. Place the cored apples in an 8 x 8-inch baking dish. Spoon some oat filling into each apple, filling all the way to the top. Pour the warm water into the baking dish around the apples. Make sure not to pour the water over the apples.

5. Bake for about 40 minutes or until the apples are slightly soft.

6. Remove the apples from the oven and, if desired, baste the outside of the apples with juices from the pan. Enjoy!

Serves: 5 | Prep and Cook Time: 1 hour

PEASANT PORRIDGE

While some kings have ambitions to conquer the entire Continent, a great divide remains in their own kingdoms. You'll often find the higher classes feasting like royalty, while poorer citizens subsist on a main dish of simple porridge.

1 cup water

¼ cup porridge oats

½ cup whole milk

½ mashed banana

1 tablespoon chia seeds, plus extra for optional topping

1 teaspoon vanilla extract

cubed strawberry, for topping (optional)

coconut chips, for topping (optional)

sliced almonds, for topping (optional)

pumpkin seeds, for topping (optional)

edible flowers, for topping (optional)

1. Place the water and oats in a medium saucepan and bring the mixture to a boil. Stir frequently until the oats start to thicken.

2. Add the milk, mashed banana, chia seeds, and vanilla extract, and cook for 4 to 5 minutes on low heat, stirring frequently to avoid burning the mixture.

3. Turn off the heat, transfer the mixture to a serving bowl, and finish the porridge with the toppings of your choice, if using.

Serves: 1 | Prep and Cook Time: 20 minutes

SIMPLE INN GROATS

The small towns scattered throughout the Continent offer few things in terms of comfort. But stop in at any small-town inn and you'll find hearty dishes like these simple-yet-satisfying groats.

2 cups toasted buckwheat groats, rinsed

1 tablespoon salt, plus extra for sprinkling

4 cups water

2 tablespoons unsalted butter

1 onion, chopped

8 to 10 cremini mushrooms, sliced

2 tablespoons chopped parsley, plus extra for serving

salt and pepper, to taste

4 slices bacon

4 eggs

1. Place the buckwheat groats in a medium pot, add the salt and water, and cook for 15 minutes, until the groats are soft and the water has evaporated.

2. Remove the pot from the heat, cover it with a lid, and let it stand for 10 to 15 minutes.

3. Put the butter, onion, and a pinch of salt in a large frying pan over medium heat. The salt will draw moisture out of the onions, which will help caramelize them.

4. When the onion has turned a darker brown, about 30 to 45 minutes of cooking, add the

mushrooms and chopped parsley and sauté for 5 minutes, adding salt and pepper to taste.

5. Add the cooked buckwheat, mix everything together, and cook the mixture for 2 more minutes. Divide the mixture between 4 serving bowls.

6. In a separate frying pan, fry the bacon and eggs. Top each bowl of groats with an egg. Chop the bacon into small pieces and sprinkle over each portion. Top the groats with extra parsley and pepper. Enjoy!

Serves: 4 | Prep and Cook Time: 1 hour to 1 hour and 25 minutes

KRAKEN STEW

In a small dukedom famous for its markets, citizens can find some of the Continent's most bizarre and rare ingredients. Magical creatures like krakens caught from the Continent's deep rivers and lakes fetch a high price at the market. But if you're too late to the market to snag some kraken for this delicious stew, lamb works well too.

4 tablespoons vegetable oil

4 tablespoons flour

1½ pounds leg of lamb, cut into cubes, excess fat trimmed

salt and pepper, to taste

1 tablespoon unsalted butter

1 onion, finely chopped

2 bay leaves

1 teaspoon fresh thyme

3 cloves garlic, minced

2 tablespoons tomato paste

2 medium potatoes, cut into wedges

4 carrots, sliced

3 cups beef stock

1 cup red wine

1. Preheat the oven to 350°F.

2. Put the oil in a large ovenproof pot over medium heat. In a bowl, mix the flour and the lamb cubes, and season the mixture with salt and pepper. Transfer the coated lamb to the pot and brown the meat. Take the lamb cubes out of the pot and set them aside in a bowl.

3. In the same pot, melt the butter. Add the onion, bay leaves, and thyme. Once the onion is translucent, add the minced garlic and sauté for 1 minute.

4. Add the tomato paste and cook for an additional minute.

5. Stir in the potatoes, carrots, and lamb. Cook for 5 minutes, stirring occasionally.

6. Add the stock and wine, and bring to a boil. Cook for 5 more minutes, and then pop the pot into the oven.

7. Cook for 1 hour and 50 minutes, or until the lamb is tender.

Note: Don't let a single bite of kraken go to waste! Store the leftovers of this and all other stew or soup recipes within for 3 to 5 days, or freeze them for up to 3 months.

Serves: 2 | Prep and Cook Time: 2 hours and 35 minutes

FISHERMAN'S STEW

In small towns that sit on the banks of rivers or the edges of oceans, the locals live their lives fishing. These waterside villages across the Continent are known for the quality of their fresh fish and, of course, their delicious and hearty fish stew.

4 cloves garlic, minced

4 anchovy fillets, minced

2 tablespoons vegetable oil

1 onion, chopped

2 ribs celery, chopped

1 carrot, chopped

½ teaspoon salt, plus extra to taste

1 (28-ounce) can diced tomatoes, with liquid

¾ cup white wine

8 ounces clam juice

3 cups water

1 pound potatoes, cut into chunks

1 bay leaf

pepper, to taste

2 pounds cod, cut in 2-inch pieces

1 cup chopped fresh parsley leaves

1. In a small bowl, use a fork to mash the minced garlic and anchovies until they are well combined. Set aside the mixture.

2. Heat the oil in a Dutch oven over medium heat. Add the onion, celery, carrot, and ½ teaspoon of salt. Cook until the onion is tender, about 5 minutes. Stir occasionally.

3. Add the pureed garlic and anchovies. Cook, stirring until the mixture is very fragrant, about 1 minute, and then add the tomatoes. Cook, stirring often until the tomatoes have cooked down a bit and the mixture smells aromatic, about 10 to 15 minutes.

4. Add the wine, clam juice, water, potatoes, bay leaf, salt, and pepper. Bring the mixture to a simmer. Turn the heat to low, partially cover the Dutch oven, and simmer the stew for 20 minutes. Taste, adjust the salt, and add pepper to taste.

5. Add the fish and simmer for 5 to 10 minutes. Remove the Dutch oven from the heat, stir in the parsley, and serve.

Serves: 4 | Prep and Cook Time: 1 hour

DWARVES' DUCK BLOOD SOUP

Dwarves are a sturdy and practical lot, and their food shares many of the same characteristics. A popular meal among the dwarves, this soup uses as much of the duck as possible, letting nothing go to waste.

2 cups fresh duck blood

½ cup vinegar

3 pounds duck parts

10 cups cold water

1 bay leaf

1 teaspoon fresh marjoram

salt and pepper, to taste

2 cups dried fruit, such as prunes, raisins, pears, apples

3 cups cooked noodles

2 cups half-and-half

4 tablespoons all-purpose flour

1. In a bowl, mix the fresh blood with the vinegar so the blood won't clot, cover the bowl, and refrigerate the mixture until it is ready to use.

2. Place the duck parts in a large pot and cover them with cold water. Bring the water to a boil, skimming off any foam that rises to the surface.

3. Add the bay leaf, marjoram, salt, and pepper. Return the mixture to a boil, reduce the heat, and simmer, partially covered, for an hour.

4. Add the dried fruit and cook the mixture for another hour. Remove the meat from the bones and return the meat to the pot. Add the noodles and heat the soup for 3 to 5 minutes.

5. Let the soup cool in an ice bath and refrigerate, if necessary, to make skimming off the fat easier and to prevent curdling once the blood and half-and-half are added.

6. When the soup is chilled, pour the half-and-half into a large bowl. Add the flour and blend it in with a fork until the mixture has a smooth texture. Add 3 ladles of cold soup and the reserved blood-vinegar mixture, and whisk the soup-vinegar mixture until it is smooth.

7. Transfer that mixture back to the pot that has the remaining soup and heat it gently until the soup is thickened and the raw flour taste is cooked out, about 15 to 20 minutes. Serve and enjoy!

Serves: 4 | Prep and Cook Time: 2 hours and 30 minutes

PRIZED POTATO SOUP

Every countryman you meet on the road will tell you that their homeland has the best cuisine. While traveling between towns, our witcher meets one such countryman who can't help but brag that his hometown makes the best potato soup on the Continent.

8 strips bacon, chopped
1 onion, chopped
2 cups sliced mushrooms
4 large russet potatoes, diced
1 clove garlic, minced
4 cups whole milk

3 cups chicken broth
2 cups potato puree
1 cup grated cheddar cheese
¾ cup sour cream or more to taste
salt and pepper, to taste
fresh thyme leaves, for garnish

1. Put the bacon in a large pot and fry it over medium-high heat, stirring occasionally, until it is nice and crispy, about 10 minutes. When the bacon is done, remove it from the pot and set it aside. Leave the bacon fat in the pot.

2. Add the onion to the pot and cook until it's translucent, about 5 minutes. Add the mushrooms and cook the mixture for 5 minutes, stirring occasionally.

3. Add the potatoes and garlic, and cook the mixture for 5 minutes, stirring frequently.

4. Pour in the milk and broth, and simmer for 20 minutes, until the potatoes are fork tender.

5. Stir in the potato puree, cheddar cheese, and sour cream. Cook the soup for 5 minutes. Season the soup with salt and pepper to taste, and add the bacon (reserve some to top the soup with).

6. Ladle the soup into bowls, topping each with some bacon and thyme. Sprinkle each bowl of soup with extra pepper. Enjoy!

Serves: 4 | Prep and Cook Time: 1 hour

BARON'S BLACK BEAN SOUP

A delicious bowl of black bean soup might be just what you need after escaping a bog full of crones and finding shelter in the manor of a mysterious baron desperately searching for his wife and daughter. Maybe sharing your soup might bring him some comfort.

1 tablespoon olive oil

1 onion, chopped

1 green bell pepper, chopped

2 jalapeño peppers, chopped

2 ribs celery, chopped

1 carrot, chopped

3 cloves garlic, chopped

1 tablespoon chili powder

1 teaspoon cayenne pepper

1 teaspoon paprika powder

1 teaspoon dried or fresh oregano

1 teaspoon cumin

red pepper flakes, to taste

salt and pepper, to taste

4 cups drained and rinsed black beans, the equivalent of 2 (15-ounce) cans

2 cups chicken broth

juice from 1 small lime

spicy chili flakes, for garnish

chopped fresh parsley, for garnish

sliced jalapeño, for garnish

1. In a large pot, heat the olive oil over medium heat. Add the onion, peppers, celery, and carrot. Cook the mixture for 10 minutes, stirring occasionally.

2. Add the garlic, chili powder, cayenne, paprika, oregano, cumin, red pepper flakes, salt, and pepper. Stir the mixture and cook for 30 seconds, until the garlic becomes fragrant.

3. Add the black beans and chicken broth, and stir to combine. Bring the mixture to a boil, then reduce the heat and simmer for 20 minutes.

4. Using an immersion blender, blend the soup for 10 to 20 seconds. Don't blend the soup too much! You can also process part of the soup in a food processor, and then mix it with the remaining soup.

5. Adjust the taste with salt and pepper. Serve the soup in bowls and swirl in some fresh lime juice. Garnish each bowl of soup with chili flakes, parsley, and sliced jalapeño and enjoy!

Serves: 4 | Prep and Cook Time: 1 hour

CRAWFISH BOIL

The Continent is full of talented chefs hard at work in grand castle kitchens or humble taverns. This delicious seafood dish is brought to you by a chef particularly famous throughout the Continent, who suggests pairing this meal with a dry white wine.

10 cups water

2 tablespoons Cajun seasoning

1 teaspoon pepper

1 head garlic, unpeeled but with cloves separated

3 ears corn, cut into 2-inch pieces

1 pound small red potatoes, halved

1 pound smoked sausage, cut into chunks

1 lemon, sliced into rounds

3 pounds crawfish

chopped fresh parsley, for garnish

1. Fill a large pot with the water. Bring the water to a boil.

2. Add the Cajun seasoning, pepper, garlic cloves, corn, potatoes, sausage, and lemon slices. Cover the pot with a lid and simmer the mixture for 10 minutes.

3. Taste the crawfish boil water. If it's too salty, add more water. If it's too bland, add more

seasonings to taste. Transfer the crawfish to the pot and cook the mixture for 3 to 4 minutes with the lid on.

4. Turn off the heat and let the crawfish soak for 10 minutes. The longer the crawfish soak, the spicier they will be. Remove all the ingredients from the pot using a strainer, sprinkle them with chopped parsley, and serve the Crawfish Boil immediately. Enjoy!

Serves: 5 | Prep and Cook Time: 1 hour

HOUSE SPECIALTY SOUP

Quaint inns in small towns rarely have a diverse menu; instead, they offer daily specials that feature whatever ingredients they have on hand. It was just the witcher's luck that on a day he arrived at a certain court inn, their house specialty that day was this surprisingly tasty yet simple cabbage-and-bean soup.

2 tablespoons olive oil

2 leeks, sliced

1 large carrot, diced

2 stalks celery, diced

3 cloves garlic, minced

1 teaspoon fresh thyme

1 teaspoon dried or fresh rosemary

1 teaspoon dried or fresh oregano

2 cups (one 15-ounce can) diced tomatoes

1 cup beer

5 cups vegetable stock

3 medium potatoes, peeled and diced

1 small cabbage, sliced

3 cups cooked white cannellini beans, drained and rinsed

salt and pepper, to taste

chopped fresh parsley, for garnish

1. In a large pot over medium-high heat, add the oil, leeks, carrot, and celery. Sauté them for 5 minutes, stirring occasionally. Add the garlic and herbs, and sauté the mixture for an additional minute, or until it is fragrant.

2. Add the tomatoes, beer, vegetable stock, potatoes, cabbage, and beans.

3. Bring the mixture to a boil, cover the pot, reduce the heat to low, and simmer for 20 to 30 minutes, or until the potatoes and cabbage are tender. Taste for seasoning, adding salt and pepper as needed.

4. Serve the soup topped with parsley. Enjoy!

Serves: 4 | Prep and Cook Time: 50 minutes to 1 hour

CATCH OF THE DAY SANDWICH

What better way to reap the benefits of your hard labor than by making a delicious meal? While the wealthier citizens of the land enjoy exquisite meals and sweet wines, hunters and fishermen are known to make their own meals out of whatever happens to fall into their traps that day. Lucky for us, today's catch can be turned into a crispy fish sandwich.

1 cup mayonnaise

3 tablespoons minced dill pickles

2 teaspoons freshly squeezed lemon juice or white wine vinegar

1 teaspoon Dijon mustard

1 tablespoon minced green onions

¼ teaspoon hot sauce (optional)

1 teaspoon minced fresh parsley (optional)

salt and pepper, to taste

vegetable oil, for frying

1 cup cornmeal

1 cup all-purpose flour

1 tablespoon baking powder

1 teaspoon salt

1 (12-ounce) bottle amber beer

2 teaspoons Tabasco sauce

2 (6-ounce) cod fillets, cut in half horizontally

4 sandwich rolls

4 sliced radishes

arugula

1. To make the tartar sauce, whisk together the mayonnaise, pickles, lemon juice or vinegar, mustard, and green onions in a medium mixing bowl. Season the mixture to taste with the hot sauce and parsley, if using, and salt and pepper. Place the sauce in an airtight container and refrigerate it for at least 30 minutes before using it.

2. Fill a deep frying pan halfway with oil and heat it to around 350°F.

3. In a large bowl, put the cornmeal, flour, baking powder, and salt, and whisk to combine. Whisk in the beer, making sure to remove any lumps. Stir in the Tabasco sauce.

4. Sprinkle the fillets with salt and pepper, and rub the fish gently. Dip each fillet in the beer batter and add each one to the hot oil, one at a time. Fry the fillet until it is brown and crispy, 3 to 4 minutes, flipping it halfway through. Fry the remaining fillets, one at a time.

5. Transfer each fried fillet to a wire rack on a baking sheet and sprinkle it with salt and pepper.

6. Spread the Tartar Sauce on the bottom and top of the sandwich rolls. Place each fillet on the bread, and top each sandwich with the sliced radishes and arugula. Enjoy!

Serves: 4 | Prep and Cook Time: 30 to 35 minutes

VENISON BURGER

There's nothing quite like a delicious burger after a long day of fighting monsters, searching for a destined child, or bantering with a beautiful mage. When the day's hunt has been particularly good (and if you arrive early enough), you might be able to snag one of these savory venison burgers before they're gone.

FOR THE GARLIC SAUCE

¼ cup mayonnaise

1 tablespoon plain Greek yogurt

1 tablespoon lemon juice

2 cloves garlic, minced

salt, to taste

FOR THE BURGER

1 cup bacon (about 8 slices), chopped
1 pound ground venison
smoked salt, to taste
freshly ground pepper
3 tablespoons unsalted butter

1 large onion, thinly sliced
2 to 4 cheese slices
2 hamburger buns, sliced
lettuce or arugula leaves
1 tomato, thinly sliced

1. To make the garlic sauce, place all sauce ingredients in a small bowl and whisk until well combined and completely smooth. Set aside.

2. Heat a frying pan over medium-high heat and add the bacon. Cook the bacon until it is crispy and golden brown. Transfer the bacon to a large bowl and leave the grease in the pan.

3. Add the ground venison, salt, and pepper to the bacon, and mix well. Using your hands, form 2 patties. Set them aside.

4. Heat the butter in the same frying pan over medium-high heat. When the butter is melted, add the sliced onion and cook until the onion is done to your liking. Remove the onion from the pan and set aside.

5. Place the patties in the frying pan and cook for 4 to 6 minutes per side depending on how well done you like your burgers. When you flip the burgers, grind some pepper over them, and then spoon a little onion on each one.

6. With about 90 seconds to go on cooking the second side of the patties, place 1 to 2 cheese slices on top of the onions on each patty and cover the pan until the patties are ready. Spread the garlic sauce on the buns in these last 90 seconds.

7. When everything is done, move the patties and buns to a plate and start building the burgers.

8. Start with the lettuce or arugula, and then the patties, tomato slices, and any leftover onion, if desired. Top each patty with the other half of the bun and serve. Enjoy!

Serves: 2 | Prep and Cook Time: 33 to 37 minutes

POOR MAN'S BOEUF BOURGUIGNON

A favorite dish among the southern countries of the Continent, boeuf bourguignon may seem like a dish that would grace only the tables of wealthy nobles and kings. However, citizens of all classes enjoy their own version of this classic dish, making it just as easy to find in a gilded banquet hall as in a modest tavern.

1 tablespoon olive oil

8 ounces thick-cut bacon (about 8 slices), cut into 1-inch chunks

3 pounds beef, cut into 2-inch chunks

salt and pepper, to taste

1 large onion, chopped

1 pound carrots, peeled and chopped into 1-inch chunks

3 cloves garlic, minced

1 tablespoon tomato paste

1 bottle red wine, such as Merlot, Pinot Noir, or Chianti

2 cups beef stock

bouquet garni (a tied bundle of fresh
thyme, bay leaf, and fresh parsley)

4 tablespoons unsalted butter and about 2
tablespoons softened unsalted butter, divided

2 pounds cremini mushrooms, divided

1 pound pearl onions, peeled

2 tablespoons all-purpose flour

fresh thyme, to serve

French bread, to serve

1. Preheat the oven to 250°F.

2. Heat the oil in a large pot or Dutch oven. Add the bacon and cook over medium-low heat until the bacon is crispy. Remove the bacon with a slotted spoon and set it aside; leave the bacon fat in the pot or Dutch oven.

3. Pat the beef dry. Season it with salt and pepper. Increase the heat to medium. In batches, sear the beef in a single layer in the bacon fat, turning the meat until it is nicely browned on all sides, about 3 to 5 minutes per batch.

4. Once all the beef is browned, add all the beef chunks back into the pot. Then add the onion and carrots to the pot and sauté until they are softened and aromatic, about 10 minutes. Add the garlic and sauté an additional minute.

5. Add the reserved bacon. Add the tomato paste, red wine, beef stock, and bouquet garni. Season the mixture with salt and pepper, and stir to combine the seasonings. Bring the mixture to a simmer, cover the pot, and place the pot in the oven. Cook it until the meat is very tender, about 2 hours.

6. Meanwhile, heat a large pan over medium heat. Add 2 tablespoons of butter. When hot, add 1 pound of the mushrooms, season them with salt and pepper, and sauté them until they are lightly browned, about 10 minutes. Remove the mushrooms from the pan and set them aside. Repeat this step with the remaining 1 pound of mushrooms and 2 more tablespoons of butter. Sauté the pearl onions in the same pan until they are lightly browned.

7. When the meat is very tender, remove the pot from the oven. Remove the bouquet garni.

8. To make a thickener, blend the 2 tablespoons of softened butter and flour in a small bowl; add more softened butter, as needed. Add the flour mixture to the pot in small amounts, stirring after each addition until it is incorporated.

9. Add the reserved mushrooms and the mushroom and pearl onion mixture to the stew.

10. Bring the pot to a simmer on the stove, and simmer the beef for 30 minutes to thicken it. Season the beef with salt and pepper to taste. Serve it with fresh thyme and French bread. Enjoy!

Serves: 4 **|** Prep and Cook Time: 3 hours and 9 minutes to 3 hours and 15 minutes

THE PEOPLE'S BREAD

It's not all drama and battles and chaos magic on the Continent. Some countries are made of softer stuff—like this brioche. Fresh, sweet, and warm, this bread reflects the gentle people of these countries and can often be found as a delicious addition to their hearty meals.

4¾ cups all-purpose flour, divided
1 tablespoon active dry yeast
¼ cup granulated sugar
1½ teaspoons salt

½ cup warm water, plus more as needed
6 eggs, room temperature
1 cup unsalted butter, room temperature
2 teaspoons sugar, plus extra to sprinkle

1. In the bowl of an electric mixer fitted with a paddle attachment, mix together 1 cup of the flour, the active dry yeast, granulated sugar, and salt. Add the water. Mix at medium speed for a couple of minutes until the mixture is well combined.

2. Add the eggs, 1 at a time. Add the next egg only when the previous egg is well incorporated. Set the mixer's speed to low. Add 2 cups of flour, a ¼ cup at a time, and mix until the dough is well combined.

3. With the mixer on medium speed, add the butter in 6 separate batches, waiting until the butter is well incorporated before adding more.

4. Set the mixer to low speed. Add 1¾ cups of flour, a ¼ cup at a time, until the dough is well combined. The dough will be very sticky when it's done.

5. Use a rubber spatula to clean the dough off the paddle and scrape the sides of the mixing bowl. Cover the dough with plastic wrap and let it rise at room temperature for 3 hours, until it doubles in size.

6. Punch and deflate the dough completely with a rubber spatula. Cover the dough with a plate and refrigerate it overnight.

7. The next day, remove the dough from the refrigerator 3 hours before you're ready to bake. Divide the dough into 2 equal pieces. On a lightly floured clean surface, shape each dough piece into plain loaves, a braid, or individual buns. Place each piece into its own 9 x 5-inch loaf pan. If you chose to make individual buns, place each bun on a lined baking tray instead.

8. Cover each loaf pan tightly with clear plastic wrap and let the dough rise at room temperature for about 2½ to 3 hours, until it doubles.

9. Preheat the oven to 350°F while the dough is rising. Bake the loaves for 37 to 40 minutes in the center of the oven. Tent the loaves with foil if the crust is getting too dark.

10. While the loaves are baking, prepare the sugar water by mixing 2 teaspoons of sugar with 1 tablespoon of water until the sugar is completely dissolved. When the bread is done, remove the loaves from the oven and immediately brush the tops of the loaves with sugar water to give them that shiny finish. Sprinkle them with more sugar.

11. Let the bread sit in the loaf pans for 5 minutes to cool before transferring the loaves from the pans to a cooling rack to cool completely. Enjoy!

Serves: 4 | Prep and Cook Time: 1 hour, plus 6 hours to rise and overnight to refrigerate

CHEF-IN-TRAINING FLAMICHE

If the culinary arts are your passion, you'll probably make your way to study at a certain academy. This academy is surrounded by some of the Continent's best inns and restaurants, the perfect setting for a culinary student to try out their latest experimental recipe—like this flamiche. The first step to conquering this dish is understanding that no, it is not a quiche, and yes, you do need to cut, rinse, and prepare the leeks just so.

FOR THE CRUST

4 tablespoons ice water, plus more if needed

½ tablespoon apple cider vinegar

1½ cups all-purpose flour

½ teaspoon salt

1 stick unsalted butter, chilled

FOR THE FILLING

2 tablespoons unsalted butter

5 medium leeks, white and light green parts, thinly sliced

salt and white pepper, to taste

8 ounces crumbled goat cheese

1 large egg, lightly beaten

1 egg yolk, lightly beaten

¼ cup heavy cream, plus more for brushing

1. To make the crust: In a small bowl, combine the ice water and cider vinegar.

2. In a food processor, add the flour, salt, and butter, and pulse until the mixture resembles coarse meal. With the machine running, slowly add the water-vinegar mixture, processing until moist clumps form. If the dough seems dry, add ice water by the teaspoonful.

3. Gather the dough into a ball and flatten it into a disk. Wrap the dough in plastic wrap and refrigerate it for about 30 minutes or more.

4. Position a rack in the center of the oven and preheat the oven to 375°F. On a lightly floured surface, use a lightly floured rolling pin to roll the dough disk to an 11- or 12-inch round that is a generous ⅛-inch thick. Carefully fold the disk in half, slide it onto the rolling pin, and transfer it to a 9-inch fluted tart pan with a removable bottom. Gently press the dough, without stretching or tearing it, to line the pan. Use light pressure to push the dough into the sides, letting the excess dough drape over the pan. Chill the dough-lined pan while you make the filling.

5. To make the filling: Melt the butter in a large saucepan over medium heat. Add the sliced leeks and a generous pinch of salt. Cook, stirring often until the leeks are quite softened but aren't yet coloring, about 10 minutes. Stir in the cheese and a pinch of white pepper. Cook the leek mixture for 2 minutes and set it aside to cool completely.

6. In a large bowl, whisk together the egg, egg yolk, and ¼ cup of heavy cream. Stir in the cooled leek mixture and a bit more salt and white pepper. Pour the mixture into the lined tart pan and spread it evenly across the bottom.

7. Set the tart pan on a rimmed baking sheet and bake the tart in the heated oven until it is lightly golden, about 45 minutes. Let the tart pan rest on a rack for at least 10 minutes before removing the tart ring. Slice the tart and serve it warm or at room temperature. Enjoy!

Serves: 4 | Prep and Cook Time: 1½ hours

BLACKSMITH DUMPLINGS

It's not every day that you meet a legendary elven swordsmith who traded his hammer for a whisk and mixing bowl. But you can be sure that his dumplings come highly recommended and are the house specialty in every inn and tavern in the city.

FOR THE SAUCE

½ cup rice vinegar
¼ cup soy sauce

sesame seeds

FOR THE DUMPLINGS

1 pound finely minced cabbage
1 tablespoon salt, divided

1 pound ground pork shoulder
1 teaspoon white pepper

3 cloves garlic, minced

1 teaspoon minced fresh ginger

3 green onions, minced

2 teaspoons sugar

1 package dumpling wrappers (40 to 50 wrappers)

vegetable oil, for cooking

½ cup water, for cooking

1. To make the sauce, combine all ingredients in a small bowl and set it aside.

2. To make the dumplings, add the cabbage and 2 teaspoons of salt to a large bowl and toss to combine. Transfer the cabbage to a fine-mesh strainer and set the strainer over the bowl. Let the cabbage stand at room temperature for 20 minutes.

3. Transfer the cabbage to the center of a clean dish towel and gather up the edges. Twist the towel to squeeze the cabbage, wringing out as much excess moisture as possible. Discard the liquid.

4. In a large bowl, combine the pork, drained cabbage, remaining salt, white pepper, garlic, ginger, green onion, and sugar. Knead the mixture and turn it with clean hands until it is homogenous and starts to feel sticky.

5. Set up a work station: a small bowl of water, a clean dish towel for wiping your fingers, a bowl with the dumpling filling, a parchment-lined rimmed baking sheet for the finished dumplings, and a stack of dumpling wrappers covered in plastic wrap.

6. To form the dumplings, hold one wrapper in the flat palm of a hand. Using a spoon, place 2 teaspoons to 1 tablespoon of the filling in the center of the wrapper, in the shape of a disk. Use the tip of the finger on your other hand to gently moisten the edge of the wrapper with water. Wipe your fingertips dry on the kitchen towel.

7. Working from one side, carefully seal the filling inside the wrapper by folding the wrapper into a crescent shape, pleating an edge as it meets the other. Transfer the finished dumplings to the parchment-lined baking sheet.

8. In a large nonstick skillet over medium heat, add 1 tablespoon of the vegetable oil and heat it until it shimmers. Add as many dumplings as will fit in a single layer and cook them, swirling the pan, until the dumplings are evenly golden brown on the bottom surface, about 1 to 2 minutes.

9. Increase heat to medium high, add ½ cup of water, and cover the skillet tightly with a lid. Let the dumplings steam for 3 minutes, and then remove the lid. Continue cooking. Swirl the pan frequently until the water has fully evaporated and the dumplings have crisped again, about 2 minutes longer (use a thin spatula to gently dislodge the dumplings if they have stuck to the bottom of the skillet). Slide the dumplings onto a plate, turning them crispy side up, and serve them immediately with the sauce. Enjoy!

Serves: 4 | Prep and Cook Time: 55 minutes to 1 hour

A TASTE OF HOME ORANGE CHICKEN

A bite from a ghoul would be deadly for any of us humans. But for a witcher, it might just trigger a vivid fever dream of a simpler time—a boy fighting imaginary dragons and spending time with his mother as they dine on succulent dishes like this roasted orange chicken.

3- to 4-pound whole chicken

salt and pepper, to taste

¾ cup orange juice concentrate

½ cup salted butter

⅓ cup orange marmalade

1 tablespoon orange zest

1 tablespoon tamari sauce

1 tablespoon chopped fresh rosemary, plus more for garnishing

1 clove garlic, minced

1 teaspoon salt

1 large orange, cut in half

fresh rosemary, for serving

1. Lightly rub the entire chicken with salt and pepper.

2. In a saucepan, combine the orange juice, butter, marmalade, orange zest, tamari sauce, rosemary, garlic, and 1 teaspoon of salt. Simmer the mixture over medium heat until the butter has melted and everything is well combined. Stir occasionally.

3. Remove the saucepan from the heat. Bring the sauce to room temperature, and then refrigerate it until the sauce solidifies into a paste.

4. Rub the entire chicken inside and out with half of the sauce and place half an orange in the chicken. Place the chicken in a roasting pan. Cut the other orange half into wedges and place them around the chicken.

5. Refrigerate the chicken for 2 to 4 hours. You should have about a half a cup of sauce left for basting.

6. Place the chicken in an oven preheated to 350°F and roast the chicken for about 1½ to 2 hours, basting as needed. If the chicken starts to get too dark after about an hour, cover it with foil until it is finished roasting. The internal temperature of the chicken should reach 165°F when fully cooked. Decorate the chicken with fresh rosemary and serve. Enjoy!

Serves: 4 | Prep and Cook Time: 2½ to 3 hours, plus 2 to 4 hours to refrigerate

THE UNOFFICIAL WITCHER COOKBOOK

CONTINENTAL CHEESE PLATTER

The Continent is home to refined cities with some of the most brilliant minds in science and the arts, along with taverns that boast some of the best food. These taverns take it up a notch. Instead of making only the usual meat pies and stews, many establishments in these fair cities lean toward serving the finer side of dining, offering exquisite wines and platters of cheese.

½ pound cheddar cheese

½ pound Brie or Camembert

½ pound blue cheese

½ cup honey

1 cup berries (strawberries, blueberries, and blackberries)

½ cup olives

½ apple, sliced

2 to 3 grape bunches

3 varieties of crackers, 1 cup each

4 to 6 ounces prosciutto

4 to 6 ounces sliced salami

1 cup nuts

dried apricots

fresh thyme

1. Place the cheeses on the board first. Cut a few slices from each cheese.

2. Place a bowl with the honey on the board. Arrange the berries, olives, and sliced apple on the board.

3. Place the grape bunches on the board and then add the crackers, placing them in groups.

4. Next, place the prosciutto, salami, and nuts on the board.

5. Fill in any gaps with the dried apricots and fresh thyme. Enjoy!

Serves: 4 | Prep and Cook Time: 10 minutes

Food for the Journey

ROADSIDE SWEET ROLLS

These sweet rolls are a treat for children and adults alike, and witchers and other adventurers often carry them as a quick snack on the path. But watch out! Roadside thieves can easily snatch these popular rolls if one isn't paying close attention to their packs.

1 tablespoon active dry yeast
3 tablespoons sugar
1½ cups warm water
1½ tablespoons unsalted butter, at room temperature, plus extra for hot rolls

1½ teaspoons salt
3 to 4 cups all-purpose flour
sesame seeds

1. In the bowl of a stand mixer, dissolve the yeast and sugar in the warm water. Let stand 5 minutes so the mixture foams.

2. Attach the dough hook to the mixer and mix in the butter, salt, and 3 cups of the flour. Once the mixture is well combined, start adding the last cup of flour, ¼ cup at a time, until the dough forms a ball, pulls away from the sides of the bowl, and is only slightly sticky to the touch. Don't add the whole cup if it's not necessary.

3. Knead the mixture for 3 minutes at medium speed. Cover the bowl with a dishcloth and allow the dough to rise until doubled. This will take about 20 to 30 minutes.

4. Gently punch down the dough and divide it into 15 pieces. Roll each piece into a ball and place each ball in a greased 9 x 13-inch baking dish. Cover and let rise until doubled, about 20 to 30 minutes. Sprinkle the dough with sesame seeds.

5. Preheat the oven to 350°F. Bake the rolls for 15 to 20 minutes or until they are golden brown.

6. Run a small cube of butter over the tops of the hot rolls. Let them cool slightly before serving. Enjoy!

Serves: 4 | Prep and Cook Time: 1 hour and 10 minutes to 1 hour and 30 minutes

WITCHER'S SPECIALTY

This dish may seem like your run-of-the-mill omelet, but there's more to the story than that. After a powerful sorceress who has captured the white-haired witcher's heart exhausts herself from casting spells, she asks the witcher to cook for her. Despite being ill-accustomed to the finer points of cooking, he manages to make her this breakfast that reminds her of home.

FOR THE OMELET

2 eggs

¼ teaspoon paprika powder

¼ teaspoon garlic powder

salt and pepper, to taste

1 tablespoon vegetable oil

FOR THE STUFFING

2 tablespoons unsalted butter

1 teaspoon vegetable oil

5 button mushrooms, sliced

¼ cup sliced green onions, plus extra to garnish

1 red pepper, chopped

1 tablespoon soy sauce

½ teaspoon dried oregano

salt and pepper, to taste

¼ cup mozzarella cheese, grated

1. To make the omelet, whisk the eggs with the paprika powder, garlic powder, salt, pepper, and oil. Set it aside.

2. To make the stuffing, add the butter and oil to a frying pan over high heat, then add the mushrooms, green onions, and red pepper. Cook the mixture for 8 to 10 minutes, stirring occasionally.

3. When the vegetables turn slightly brown, add soy sauce, oregano, salt, and pepper. Cook for 1 minute and remove the mixture from the pan.

4. In the same pan, on low-medium heat, add the egg mixture. Cook it for 3 to 4 minutes, then flip the omelet carefully with a big spatula.

5. On ½ of the omelet, place the mushroom stuffing and top with cheese.

6. Carefully fold the other half of the omelet over the stuffing, making a semicircle.

7. Lower the heat and cover the pan so that the cheese melts.

8. Put the omelet on a plate and garnish it with extra green onions. Enjoy!

Serves: 1 | Prep and Cook Time: 20 to 25 minutes

BANDIT'S BAGUETTE

What's a sandwich with fancy cheese doing in your stockpile of food for roughing it across countries in search of adventure? Well, it might be good to know that some roadside bandits throughout the Continent turn up their noses at simple foods. Instead of settling for hard loaves of bread or a block of stale cheese, these thieves will wait around for travelers who might have more sophisticated fare on hand, like this baguette sandwich with Camembert—a soft, creamy cheese that is definitely worth waiting for.

1 baguette

4 tablespoons unsalted butter, room temperature

salt and pepper, to taste

2 tablespoons fig jam

2 tablespoons mustard

4 ounces Jambon de Paris (a type of ham), thinly sliced

3 ounces Camembert, cut lengthwise into ¼-inch-thick slices

1 cup arugula

1. Slice the baguette in half lengthwise, cutting it about ¾ of the way through.

2. Evenly coat the cut sides of the baguette with the butter and season it with salt and pepper.

3. Spread the fig jam and mustard over the butter on both sides.

4. Layer the Jambon de Paris, Camembert, and arugula onto the bottom half of the baguette.

5. Fold over the top half of the baguette and press the baguette gently to close it.

6. Cut the sandwich into the desired number of pieces and serve. Enjoy!

Serves: 2 | Prep and Cook Time: 5 minutes

TROLL'S MYSTERY STEW

Witchers aren't the only ones who are hungry on the road. Take care not to run into any trolls while you journey across the Continent, or you may get closer to a stew like this one than you would like to. Trolls will make a meal from whatever, or whoever, they can find.

1 cup, plus 1 tablespoon all-purpose flour, divided

1½ pounds beef chuck, cut into 1-inch cubes

¼ cup vegetable or olive oil

3 stalks celery, cut into 1-inch chunks

3 carrots, cut into 1-inch chunks

3 yellow or white onions, cut into 1-inch chunks

2 cups red wine

1 (14.5-ounce) can diced tomatoes

water

2 bay leaves

salt and pepper, to taste

chopped fresh parsley, for serving

1. Place 1 cup of the flour on a plate and dredge the beef on all sides. Shake off the excess and set the beef aside.

2. Heat the oil in a large pot over medium-high heat and then add the beef. Cook the beef for 5 to 10 minutes, stirring occasionally, until it is browned on all sides. Remove the beef from the pot and set it aside.

3. Add the celery, carrots, and onions to the pot. Cook for 5 minutes, or until the onions are translucent, stirring occasionally.

4. Add the remaining 1 tablespoon of flour and stir for 1 minute. Add the wine and tomatoes. Fill the tomato can with water and add the water to the pot. Add the bay leaves and beef, and then season the mixture with salt and pepper. Cover the pot and cook the beef over low heat for about 40 minutes, stirring occasionally, until the meat is tender.

5. Remove the bay leaves, and then sprinkle the stew with chopped parsley and enjoy!

Serves: 4 | Prep and Cook Time: 55 minutes to 1 hour

REFUGEE STEW

Sometimes a meal on the road isn't one you planned. When fleeing from invading forces, a young princess haunted by destiny disguises herself as a peasant and takes shelter with a group of refugees on the road whose appetites are not quite as refined as those she is accustomed to. But a good hot stew like this one, full of hearty meats and vegetables, is just what any princess needs to regain her strength after her kingdom has fallen.

1 tablespoon olive oil

1 pound kielbasa sausage, halved and thinly sliced

1 onion, diced

2 carrots, diced

2 stalks celery, thinly sliced

1 tablespoon salt, divided

1 teaspoon pepper, divided

2 tablespoons tomato paste

3 cloves garlic, minced

6 cups low-sodium beef broth

2 medium red potatoes, peeled and diced

1 medium sweet potato, peeled and diced

1 (15-ounce) can fire-roasted diced tomatoes, with the juice

1 (15-ounce) can chickpeas, drained and rinsed

1 tablespoon finely chopped fresh rosemary

3 ounces kale, stems removed and torn into small pieces

1. To a large pot over medium heat, add the oil and when it's hot, add the sausage. Cook for 5 to 7 minutes. Use a spoon to remove the sausage and set it aside.

2. Add the onion, carrots, and celery. Add 1 teaspoon of the salt and ½ teaspoon of the pepper. Cook for 5 to 10 minutes, stirring occasionally or until the vegetables start to soften. Stir in the tomato paste and garlic, and cook for 2 minutes.

3. Add the beef broth, red potatoes, sweet potato, diced tomatoes and their juice, chickpeas, rosemary, and the remaining salt and pepper.

4. Stir the soup, cover the pot, and bring the soup to a simmer. Reduce the heat to medium low and cook the soup for 30 minutes or until the vegetables are fork tender.

5. Uncover the pot and add the browned sausage. Stir in the kale and cook for 5 to 10 minutes or until the greens are wilted.

6. Taste for seasoning and add more salt and pepper, if needed. Ladle the soup into bowls and sprinkle the soup with extra pepper, if desired. Serve the soup with crusty bread or crackers for dunking.

Serves: 4 | Prep and Cook Time: 1 hour to 1 hour and 10 minutes

DESERTER'S CHICKEN SANDWICH

When two countries battle for control, there are bound to be deserters from both sides who grow tired of the fighting and turn into bandits on the road. Outside of what they can steal, food is scarce, but they somehow always manage to have a chicken sandwich on them.

5 tablespoons mustard, divided

2 tablespoons olive oil

½ teaspoon onion powder

1 tablespoon barbecue sauce

salt and pepper, to taste

2 chicken breasts

4 tablespoons sour cream

3 fresh basil leaves, minced

1 clove garlic, minced

zest from 1 lemon

2 ciabatta buns, halved

1 tomato, sliced

2 large lettuce leaves

1. To a large bowl, add 3 tablespoons of the mustard, olive oil, onion powder, barbecue sauce, salt, and pepper. Mix well and add the chicken breasts. Toss until the breasts are well coated. Cover and refrigerate for 1 hour.

2. In a small bowl, stir together the sour cream, basil, garlic, lemon zest, 2 tablespoons of the mustard, and salt and pepper to taste. Stir well and set aside. This is the aioli.

3. Preheat the grill to medium-high heat and grill the chicken breasts for about 5 minutes per side or until they are no longer pink in the center.

4. Spread the aioli on both sides of the buns and top the bottom half of each bun with the grilled chicken, sliced tomato, and lettuce. Cover each sandwich with the top half of the bun. Enjoy!

Serves: 2 | Prep and Cook Time: 20 minutes, plus 1 hour to refrigerate

HAM AND GRAVY FROM THE BLACK FOREST

When traveling through a certain dark forest, the witcher happens upon an exquisite feast of ham and gravy. This meal is not the result of a hunt, however. No, this ham and gravy magically appear in a mysterious manor, a feast ready to be eaten. Who's to say if this meal is cursed or made of more friendly magic…?

½ cup brown sugar

¼ cup honey

¼ cup orange juice

1 teaspoon yellow mustard

½ teaspoon pepper

pinch of ground nutmeg

pinch of ground cinnamon

1 (2-pound) ham

2 cups water

2 tablespoons cornstarch dissolved in ¼ cup water

1. Preheat your oven to 350°F.

2. In a small bowl, mix together the brown sugar, honey, orange juice, mustard, pepper, nutmeg, and cinnamon. This is the glaze.

3. Score the ham by making diagonal cuts in the fat along the sides of the ham at approximately 1-inch intervals. Then turn the ham and repeat the cuts diagonally from one side to the other to form diamond shapes.

4. Place the ham, fat side facing up, in a plastic roasting bag and spoon the glaze over the top of the ham. Secure the bag and roast the

ham until it reaches at least a 130°F internal temperature, or until the crust turns golden, about 1 hour.

5. Remove the ham from the bag and put it on a plate. Pour the ham drippings into a saucepan over medium heat. Add the water and the cornstarch mixture.

6. Simmer, whisking continuously until the sauce starts to thicken. If needed, season it with additional salt and pepper, and then remove the saucepan from the heat and transfer the sauce to a gravy boat. Serve the sauce with the ham and enjoy!

Serves: 6 | Prep and Cook Time: 1 hour and 30 minutes

MOUNTAIN MEAT PIES

It's no secret that the mountains can be very dangerous places, but traveling through them can be worth it. Mountains offer plenty of game to hunt, perfect for cooking up hearty meat pies and sharing them with your troubadour friend who just can't seem to stay out of trouble.

1 tablespoon olive oil
1 onion, finely diced
2 ribs celery, chopped
1 pound ground pork
1 pound ground beef
2 cups hot beef broth
1 cup red wine
2 cups cubed potatoes

½ teaspoon ground nutmeg
1 tablespoon fresh thyme
2 cloves garlic, minced
2 tablespoons Worcestershire sauce
salt and pepper, to taste
2 sheets fresh puff pastry
1 egg

1. Heat the olive oil in a large pot over medium heat and add the onion and celery. Cook for 5 minutes or until the onion is translucent. Stir occasionally.

2. Add the pork and beef and cook for 5 minutes, stirring frequently, until the meat is browned.

3. Pour in the beef broth, red wine, and potatoes, and simmer for 10 minutes. Add the nutmeg, thyme, garlic, Worcestershire sauce, salt, and pepper. Continue cooking until the potatoes are fork tender and the liquid in the

mixture has evaporated. Set the mixture aside to cool completely.

4. Preheat the oven to 400°F. Cut the puff pastry into squares and line 15 to 20 mini pie cavities or muffin tins with the puff pastry. Then fill each with the meat mixture. Top with some more puff pastry squares, roll the edges under, and pinch around the entire pie. Use a sharp knife to slice a slit in the top of each pie.

5. Whisk 1 egg well to make an egg wash. Brush each pie with the egg wash. Bake the pies until the crusts are golden brown, about 20 minutes. Enjoy!

Serves: 10 | Prep and Cook Time: 1 hour

THE UNOFFICIAL WITCHER COOKBOOK

CAMPFIRE ROASTED RABBIT

Hunting monsters in the wilderness doesn't always allow for a fine dining experience. At the end of a long day of travel, you'll find many a witcher roasting over the campfire whatever fresh game they caught that day. If you don't have a campfire readily available to make this dish, an oven will do just fine.

2 tablespoons mustard

3 tablespoons apple cider vinegar

2 tablespoons Worcestershire sauce

2 tablespoons honey

1 teaspoon garlic powder

1 teaspoon onion powder

3 cloves garlic, minced

1 tablespoon chopped fresh rosemary

1 tablespoon chopped fresh thyme

½ cup unsalted butter, at room temperature

salt and pepper, to taste

1 whole rabbit

3 onions, quartered

8 to 10 baby potatoes, halved (or 2 large potatoes, sliced)

4 carrots, sliced roughly

¼ cup white wine

1. In a medium bowl, add the mustard, vinegar, Worcestershire sauce, honey, garlic powder, onion powder, minced garlic, rosemary, thyme, butter, salt, and pepper. Stir the mixture until the ingredients are well combined.

2. Rub the rabbit with the butter mixture, put it on a baking tray, and refrigerate for 2 hours.

3. Preheat the oven to 400°F. Place the vegetables around the rabbit and pour on the wine. Sprinkle the rabbit with salt and pepper, and cover the baking tray with aluminum foil.

4. Bake the rabbit for 1 hour, or until the meat is falling apart. Remove the foil and bake for an extra 10 to 15 minutes. Serve and enjoy!

Serves: 2 | Prep and Cook Time: 1 hour and 15 minutes, plus 2 hours to refrigerate

SALAD ON THE PATH

When you have embarked on a dangerous journey on long roads and through forgotten forests, a leafy salad may not be the first food you'd expect for a repast during the trip. But when game is scarce, a witcher must turn to the forest for food, gathering leaves and nuts to make a hearty meal.

3 fresh beets
4 cups mixed salad greens
1 cup watercress

½ orange, sliced
½ cup toasted hazelnuts, roughly chopped
½ cup shaved parmesan cheese

FOR THE VINAIGRETTE

3 tablespoons olive oil
1 teaspoon fresh orange zest
2 tablespoons orange juice
1 tablespoon white wine vinegar
2 teaspoons honey

1 teaspoon Dijon mustard
½ teaspoon salt
½ teaspoon pepper
2 tablespoons minced fresh tarragon

1. Preheat the oven to 425°F. Scrub the beets and trim their tops. Wrap each beet in foil and place them on a baking sheet.

2. Bake them for 50 to 60 minutes or until they tender. Remove the foil and cool the beets completely. Peel the beets and cut them into wedges or cubes.

3. To make the vinaigrette, in a small bowl, whisk the oil, orange zest, orange juice, vinegar, honey, mustard, salt, and pepper until blended. Stir in the tarragon.

4. In a large bowl, combine the salad greens and watercress. Drizzle with the vinaigrette and toss gently to coat the greens.

5. Transfer the salad to a platter and top it with the orange slices and beets. Sprinkle the salad with the toasted hazelnuts and cheese shavings. Serve the salad immediately.

Serves: 2 | Prep and Cook Time: 1 hour to 1 hour and 10 minutes

BASIC BUTTER NOODLES

Witchers need to excel at many things: sword fighting, hand-to-hand combat, and even a bit of magic. Between training and studying to become a witcher, witchers-in-training still have their basic chores to tend to, including preparing meals (whether they can cook or not). It's no surprise that some young witchers can cook only the most basic of dishes: butter noodles.

1 tablespoon plus ½ teaspoon salt

8 ounces fettuccine

2 tablespoons unsalted butter

3 cloves garlic, minced

¼ teaspoon red pepper flakes

¼ cup vegetable stock

1 cup heavy cream

⅓ cup freshly grated parmesan cheese

pepper, to taste

fresh parsley, chopped

1. Bring a large pot of water to a rolling boil, and then add 1 tablespoon of salt and the pasta. Cook just to al dente, according to the package directions, and then drain the fettuccine and set it aside.

2. In a large skillet over medium-high heat, melt the butter. Stir in the garlic and red pepper flakes, followed by the vegetable stock. Bring the mixture to a simmer and cook it for 1 to 2 minutes.

3. Stir in the heavy cream and cook the mixture for 1 to 2 minutes, until the cream is thickened slightly. Add the parmesan cheese, ½ teaspoon salt, and pepper. Stir well.

4. Add the drained pasta to the sauce, toss gently to coat, and sprinkle the pasta with parsley. Serve right away and enjoy!

Serves: 2 | Prep and Cook Time: 20 to 25 minutes

FISHING FOR A DJINN

Hunting beasts doesn't always involve a sword, and neither does fighting them; sometimes, all a witcher needs is a fishing pole. Be careful of the rivers you fish in. Instead of providing you with a delicious meal of baked catfish, your fishing adventures might just end with an angry djinn caught on your hook and a bard who can no longer sing.

3 tablespoons extra-virgin olive oil, divided

½ cup cornmeal

1 tablespoon Cajun seasoning

2 catfish fillets

salt and pepper, to taste

lemon wedges, for serving

1. Preheat the oven to 425°F. Drizzle 1 tablespoon of the oil on a large baking sheet.

2. In a deep plate, combine the cornmeal and Cajun seasoning. Season the catfish with salt and pepper, and then dredge the fish in the seasoned cornmeal. Press the coating onto the fish so the fish is well coated.

3. Place the fish on the prepared baking sheet and drizzle the fish with the remaining oil. Bake the fish until it is golden and flakes easily with a fork, about 15 minutes. Serve the fish with the lemon wedges and enjoy!

Serves: 2 | Prep and Cook Time: 20 minutes

VENISON JERKY

You can't traverse the Continent looking for monsters to hunt without dried meat to snack on. Luckily (for the witcher, at least), in a fight between a witcher and a beast, animals like deer may get caught in the cross fire. It's best not to let the meat go to waste!

1 pound boneless venison roast
½ cup soy sauce
½ cup Worcestershire sauce
2 tablespoons brown sugar

1 teaspoon garlic powder
2 teaspoons pepper
1 teaspoon onion powder
¼ cup dark beer

1. Slice the venison against the grain into thin, long strips.

2. In a large ziplock bag, combine the remaining ingredients to make a marinade. Stir the mixture until it is well combined.

3. Add the sliced venison and close the bag. Place the bag in the refrigerator for 24 hours.

4. Preheat a dehydrator to 170°F.

5. Remove the bag from the refrigerator, remove the venison slices from the bag, and pat each slice dry.

6. Put the venison slices on the dehydrator rack. Cook the venison for 3 to 5 hours. After 2 hours, check every slice because the cooking time can vary a bit depending on the thickness of the slices.

7. When the jerky is firm but still flexible, remove the slices from the dehydrator. Transfer the slices to a ziplock bag to cool, leaving it partially open. This helps the jerky retain some necessary moisture. Once the slices are fully cooled, transfer the jerky to the refrigerator, where it can be stored for up to 6 months.

Serves: 2 | Prep and Cook Time: 3 to 5 hours, plus 24 hours to marinate

WILD BOAR ROAST

A feast of wild boar isn't your typical fare on the road. But when you are resting and recovering your strength between monster hunts, it can be easy to tag along with the nearby village hunting expedition for a little light exercise. It also gives you the chance to impress the villagers when you slay a charging boar in one fell swoop.

1 onion, roughly chopped

4 cloves garlic, minced and divided

2 carrots, roughly chopped

2 stalks celery, roughly chopped

2 medium potatoes, roughly chopped

½ cup olive oil, divided

salt and pepper, to taste

1½ pounds wild boar roast

2 tablespoons finely chopped fresh thyme

2 tablespoons finely chopped fresh rosemary

2 tablespoons finely chopped fresh oregano

½ cup vegetable stock

1. Heat the oven to 375°F.

2. In a large bowl, toss the onion, 2 minced cloves of garlic, carrots, celery, potatoes, and ¼ cup of the olive oil. Season the mixture with salt and pepper. Put the mixture in a small roasting pan and set it aside.

3. Heat a skillet on high heat until it is very hot. Season the roast with salt and pepper. Add a tablespoon of the olive oil to the skillet and sear the roast on all sides.

4. While the meat is searing, place the chopped herbs in a small bowl and add the remainder of the minced garlic and olive oil. Stir the mixture to form a loose paste.

5. After the boar has been seared, rub it all over with the paste and place it over the vegetables in the roasting pan.

6. Add vegetable stock to the pan, and then cover the pan and roast the meat for 30 minutes, or as long as it takes for the meat to reach an internal temperature of 160°F.

7. Allow the meat to rest for about 5 minutes before slicing it and serving it with the roasted vegetables.

Serves: 6 | Prep and Cook Time: 45 minutes to 1 hour

FEASTS FIT FOR A KING

DUCK CONFIT

It's no surprise that a dish as rich in flavor as duck confit is a favorite to be served in the gilded halls of the Continent. This dish usually sits somewhere between the dry wines and sweet desserts, and is particularly enjoyed for its savory meat that practically falls off the bone.

4 duck legs

1 tablespoon salt

1 tablespoon garam masala

3 cloves garlic

1 teaspoon coriander seeds

10 juniper berries

2 bay leaves

1 tablespoon herbes de Provence

4 cups duck fat, or more if needed

fresh greens for serving

chutney, for serving

1. Toss the duck legs with the salt and garam masala to coat them as evenly as possible. Refrigerate the legs for at least 3 hours or preferably overnight.

2. When you are ready to cook the duck, preheat the oven to 275°F. To make a bouquet garni, wrap the garlic, coriander seeds, juniper berries, bay leaves, and herbes de Provence in cheesecloth to make a pouch.

3. In a medium ovenproof pot with a lid, melt the duck fat in the oven. Make sure the pot can hold the duck legs snugly. Immerse the legs in the melted fat. They must be fully immersed. If not, add more fat.

4. Place the bouquet garni in the pot, cover, and bake for 3 hours until the duck legs have shrunk somewhat, are browned, and the bottoms of the leg bones are exposed.

5. If you will be serving the duck later, let the legs cool and then refrigerate the duck legs in the fat. Making a confit is a traditional preserving technique, and the legs can stay refrigerated in the fat for up to 6 months.

6. When you are ready to serve the duck legs, remove the legs from the fat. Sauté them in a bit of the fat until they are warmed through and the skin is crisp. Serve the duck with the fresh greens and chutney.

Serves: 4 | Prep and Cook Time: 3 hours and 10 minutes, plus 3 hours to overnight to refrigerate

CHEF'S KISS PASTA

A simple pasta can be elevated to the most regal of dishes with the right ingredients. This particular pasta recipe has been perfected by a famous chef known throughout the Continent, making it a favorite at the tables of nobles.

1 pound tagliatelle pasta

2 tablespoons olive oil

2 tablespoons unsalted butter

1 onion, finely diced

2 cloves garlic, minced

1 cup cherry tomatoes, halved

1 teaspoon garlic powder

salt and pepper, to taste

1½ cups diced leftover cooked turkey

3 tablespoons white wine

¼ cup hot chicken stock

1 cup heavy cream

1 cup ricotta cheese

2 cups arugula

2 tablespoons freshly grated parmesan cheese

1. Bring water to a boil in a large pot and add the pasta. Cook the pasta al dente, according to the instructions on the package. Drain the pasta and set it aside.

2. In a large pot over medium heat, add the olive oil and butter. When the oil is hot, add the onion and cook it until it is translucent, about 5 minutes. Stir in the minced garlic, tomatoes, garlic powder, salt, and pepper. Sauté the mixture for a few minutes.

3. Stir in the diced turkey and wine. Cook for 2 minutes and then add the chicken stock, heavy cream, and ricotta cheese. Simmer the mixture for 2 minutes, stirring frequently.

4. Stir in the pasta and season with extra salt and pepper. Add the arugula and toss gently. Serve the pasta with grated parmesan.

Serves: 2 | Prep and Cook Time: 30 to 35 minutes

SWEET-AND-SOUR PORK CHOPS

A princess marrying her true love should be a reason to celebrate! But just like these pork chops, this engagement announcement was both sweet and sour. Not everyone was happy that the princess cast aside many a prince and noble in favor of a cursed knight. Unfortunately, these pork chops didn't survive such a tumultuous betrothal banquet, but maybe you'll have better luck in your own kitchen.

2 bone-in pork loin rib chops

2½ cups apple cider, divided

1 cup water

½ cup kosher salt

1 large apple, chopped

1 onion, finely diced

4 cloves garlic, minced

1 teaspoon canola or other neutral oil

4 sprigs fresh thyme

1. Prick the pork chops all over with a fork. Flip the pork chops and prick the other side of the chops.

2. Place 2 cups of the apple cider, water, and kosher salt in a gallon-size ziplock bag. Seal the bag and massage it to dissolve the salt. Add the pork chops and seal the bag again.

3. Place the bag on a rimmed baking sheet and arrange the pork chops so they sit in a single layer. Let the chops brine at room temperature for 30 minutes or refrigerate them for up to 8 hours.

4. When you are ready to cook the chops, core the apple and cut it and the onion into wedges, and smash the garlic.

5. Remove the pork chops from the brine and pat them dry with paper towels.

6. Heat a large cast-iron skillet over medium-high heat until it just begins to smoke. Add the pork chops and cook them until they begin to brown, about 1 minute on each side.

7. Reduce the heat to medium. Continue to cook the chops, flipping them every minute, until they register 145°F in the thickest part of the chops, 6 to 8 minutes more. Transfer the pork chops to a plate.

8. Add 1 teaspoon canola or other neutral oil to the pan. Add the onion, garlic, and thyme, and cook until the onion begins to soften and brown, 3 to 4 minutes. Add the apples and the remaining ½ cup of apple cider, and nestle the chops on top. Cook the chops until the apples are warm and tender but not falling apart, 3 to 4 minutes. Enjoy!

Serves: 2 | Prep and Cook Time: 20 minutes, plus 30 minutes to 8 hours to brine

FEAST OF HAM AND NIGHTSHADE

Mages are sent to kingdoms across the Continent to provide wisdom, magic, and strategy to their new kings. But when a certain mage is tired of the disrespect and politics of the generals in her court, she takes their power for herself over a feast of ham and nightshade, cleverly masking the deadly nightshade with the taste of alcohol.

7-pound smoked bone-in ham

12 ounces dark beer

1½ cups brown sugar

¼ cup maple syrup

2 tablespoons stone-ground mustard

2 tablespoons coconut aminos or soy sauce

1 tablespoon cornstarch

2 teaspoons allspice

1 tablespoon smoked paprika

salt and pepper, to taste

1. Preheat the oven to 350°F and line a large, rimmed baking sheet with foil. Place an oven-safe oven rack on top.

2. Place the ham on the rack and score the ham by making diagonal cuts in the fat along the sides of the ham, cutting down about ½ inch. Then turn the ham and repeat the cuts diagonally from one side to the other to form diamond shapes.

3. In a medium bowl, whisk together the beer, brown sugar, maple syrup, mustard, coconut aminos or soy sauce, cornstarch, salt, allspice, smoked paprika, and pepper. Taking about ⅓ of the mixture, brush it on the entire ham generously.

4. Place the ham in the oven, uncovered, and bake it for 1 hour. Remove it from the oven, brush another ⅓ of the glaze on top, and place the ham back in the oven. Bake it for an additional hour or until the top is brown and crisp. Remove the ham from the oven and set it aside.

5. In a small saucepan, add the remaining ⅓ of the glaze. Heat it over medium-low heat until the alcohol has cooked out and the glaze is thick. Remove the saucepan from the heat and pour the glaze into a serving bowl.

6. Slice the ham and serve it warm with the glaze. Enjoy!

Serves: 6 | Prep and Cook Time: 2½ hours

FROM EGGS TO APPLES

This odd yet delicious dish is a favorite combination among certain nobles. A royal feast can't be a fully complete royal feast without a dish of eggs followed by sweet apples for dessert. The more eggs and apples there are, the better!

4 eggs
2 large apples, sliced into wedges
3 to 5 tablespoons maple syrup

¾ teaspoon vanilla extract
1 teaspoon ground cinnamon

1. Preheat the oven to 350°F.

2. To make the eggs, bring a small pot with water to a boil, then reduce the water to a simmer. Gently lower the eggs into the water with a spoon. Simmer them for 6 to 7 minutes (6 minutes for a very runny yolk and 7 minutes for a still runny and barely starting to set yolk).

3. Meanwhile, prepare a bowl filled with water and ice cubes. When the eggs are done, immediately place them in the ice bath and let them cool completely.

4. To prepare the apples, place them in a deep baking dish. Drizzle them with the maple syrup and vanilla. Sprinkle them with cinnamon and toss them so they're well coated with the cinnamon.

5. Bake the apples for 10 to 15 minutes or until they're fork tender. Serve them with the soft-boiled eggs and enjoy!

Serves: 2 | Prep and Cook Time: 24 to 30 minutes

FEAST FOR A BEAST

You might just find a meal fit for a king where you least expect it. The white-haired witcher found this delicious roast when he was traveling through the countryside. He happened upon a beast who was all too eager to dine with a guest. Some days, a beast may try to make you his meal, but other days a beast will invite you to one.

1 teaspoon smoked paprika

2 tablespoons, plus ½ cup olive oil

2 teaspoons salt, plus more as needed

2 teaspoons freshly ground pepper, plus more as needed

2 pounds tri-tip steak

3 cloves garlic, minced

2 cups finely chopped fresh parsley

½ cup finely chopped cilantro

¼ cup red wine vinegar

1 tablespoon maple syrup

1. In a small bowl, mix the paprika, 2 tablespoons of olive oil, 2 teaspoons of salt, and 2 teaspoons of pepper. Rub the mixture over the steak and let the steak sit at room temperature for 30 minutes.

2. Meanwhile, prepare a grill for medium-high, indirect heat. For a charcoal grill, bank the coals on one side. For a gas grill, leave one of two burners off.

3. Place the steak over the indirect heat, cover the grill, and grill the steak, turning it once, until an instant-read thermometer inserted into the thickest part of the steak registers 115°F, about 20 to 30 minutes.

4. Move the steak to the direct heat and grill it until it's lightly charred, about 2 minutes per side. Transfer the steak to a cutting board and let it rest for 10 minutes before slicing it against the grain.

5. While the steak is resting, make the chimichurri sauce by combining the garlic, parsley, cilantro, red wine vinegar, maple syrup, and the remaining ½ cup of olive oil. Season the sauce with salt and pepper. Serve the steak with the chimichurri sauce and enjoy!

Serves: 4 | Prep and Cook Time: 40 to 60 minutes, plus 30 minutes to marinate

WITCHER'S QUAIL

A once-noble man cursed to live as a beast still maintains the reputation of his dining hall when he has guests. When a certain witcher finds his way to the beast's dilapidated mansion, this beast prepares for his guest a rich and magical meal of roasted venison, truffles, wine, and an exquisite dish of quail.

2 firm sour apples
1 carrot, peeled and diced
1 stalk celery, diced
2 shallots, diced
1 tablespoon olive oil
1 cup sourdough bread crumbs
¼ cup chicken stock

4 tablespoons unsalted butter, melted
2 sprigs fresh thyme
½ cup pecans, half roughly chopped, divided
coarse salt and freshly ground pepper, to taste
2 quails, rinsed and patted dry
1 tablespoon canola or olive oil
mixed greens and balsamic glaze, for serving

1. Preheat the oven to 450°F.

2. Quarter and core the apples. Dice half of them and set them aside. Thinly slice the remaining apples lengthwise and set them aside.

3. To a heavy ovenproof sauté pan, add the carrot, celery, shallots, and diced apples. Drizzle the mixture with olive oil and bake for 10 minutes or until softened. Transfer the mixture to a bowl and add the bread crumbs, and then add the chicken stock, 1 tablespoon of melted butter, thyme, and one half of the pecans (chopped), and toss the mixture with your hands to combine. Season the mixture with salt and pepper.

4. Sprinkle the cavity of each quail with salt and pepper and then stuff them with the bread crumb mixture. Save the leftover mixture. Season the outside of the quail with salt and pepper and truss them with kitchen string.

5. Put the quail in the same heavy ovenproof pan, and drizzle them with the remaining 3 tablespoons of butter. Bake the quail for 7 to 8 minutes. Turn them over and bake them for an additional 8 to 10 minutes. The breast meat should still be a rosy color.

6. Meanwhile, in a medium bowl, toss the mixed greens with the remaining apples and pecans and just enough balsamic glaze to coat the greens.

7. Remove the string from the quail. Arrange the salad on serving plates and place the quail alongside the salad. Add the remaining filling to the plate. Enjoy!

Serves 2 | Prep and Cook Time: 40 to 43 minutes

SEARED GORGON STEAK

The gorgon is a dangerous, venomous monster that even witchers do their best to avoid. But for a princess who has spent most of her childhood living as a vicious, cursed beast who stalked the streets on the full moon, gorgons are just another meal. After her curse is lifted, this princess now prefers her meat on the rare side.

1 (1-pound) rib eye steak
1 tablespoon olive oil
salt and pepper, to taste
4 tablespoons unsalted butter, room temperature

1 clove garlic, minced
1 sprig fresh rosemary
1 sprig fresh thyme

1. Allow the steak to come to room temperature. Pat the steak thoroughly dry using paper towels. Heat a cast-iron skillet on high for 3 to 5 minutes or until the skillet is warm; add the oil.

2. Season the steak with salt and pepper. Sear the steak for 2 to 3 minutes, and flip and sear the other side for 2 to 3 minutes.

3. After both sides are seared, turn the heat down to medium low and add the butter, garlic, rosemary, and thyme.

4. Once the butter is melted, turn the steak a third time and cook for an additional 1 minute. Using a spoon, scoop and drizzle the butter mixture over the steak.

5. Then turn the steak a fourth time and cook for an additional 1 minute while you scoop and drizzle the butter mixture over the steak.

6. Test the temperature using a meat thermometer. The temperature for a rare steak is 130°F to 135°F.

7. Remove the steak to a cutting board to rest for 5 minutes. This resting is important to allow the steak to reabsorb some juices and cook a little more from the residual heat.

8. After the steak rests, cut into half-inch slices across the grain and enjoy!

Serves: 2 | Prep and Cook Time: 15 to 20 minutes

SPICED LAMB CHOPS

Between his travels, the witcher reunites with an old sorceress friend over a dinner of exquisite meats and spices and only the finest wines. While it's not uncommon for the most delicious of meals like this one to be made with the help of a little magic, these lamb chops are as authentic as they come. Even though there is no magic in this food, there is still more to this dinner than what meets the eye.

8 lamb rib chops

1 heaping tablespoon Mina Harissa Spicy Moroccan Red Pepper Sauce

4 tablespoons extra-virgin olive oil

½ lemon, juice and zest

3 cloves garlic, minced

1 tablespoon finely chopped cilantro, plus extra to garnish

1 tablespoon finely chopped mint

½ teaspoon ground cinnamon

½ teaspoon allspice

½ teaspoon cumin powder

½ teaspoon ginger powder

½ to 1 teaspoon cayenne pepper

salt and pepper, to taste

1. Wash and pat the chops dry. Place them in a shallow dish.

2. Whisk together all the remaining ingredients, except for the cilantro reserved for the garnish, in a small bowl until they are well combined.

3. Divide half the marinade between the 8 chops, using a spoon to drizzle it over the surface of each chop. Flip the chops over and spoon the remaining marinade over them. Cover the dish with plastic wrap and refrigerate it for at least 6 hours, preferably overnight.

4. When you are ready to cook the chops, preheat the oven to 400°F. Place the chops in a baking tray and bake them for 20 minutes or until they are ready. Sprinkle them with chopped cilantro and serve. Enjoy!

Serves: 4 | Prep and Cook Time: 30 minutes, plus 6 hours to overnight to marinate

ROASTED ROYAL TURKEY

A king's table is often filled with exquisite food, such as meat brought in from the kingdom's most skilled hunters. If you're lucky enough to be a part of such a grand meal, you may see a fair share of wild boar, deer, and golden-brown, roasted turkey, a personal favorite of a certain king who is harboring a dark secret.

FOR THE TURKEY

1 (10-pound) turkey, preferably free range or organic

salt and pepper, to taste

olive oil

1 cup salted butter, softened

1 teaspoon ground sage

1 teaspoon finely chopped fresh rosemary

1 teaspoon finely chopped fresh thyme

½ teaspoon freshly ground pepper, for the flavored butter

1 clementine, halved

few sprigs of fresh rosemary

2 carrots, roughly chopped

1 large orange, roughly chopped

3 Granny Smith apples, roughly chopped

2 sticks celery, roughly chopped

2 potatoes, roughly chopped

2 tablespoons all-purpose flour

4 cups organic chicken or vegetable stock

FOR THE STUFFING

olive oil

2 onions, peeled and finely chopped

sea salt and freshly ground pepper

½ teaspoon ground nutmeg

few sprigs of fresh sage, leaves picked and roughly chopped

1 cup ground pork

1 large handful bread crumbs

1. Take the turkey out of the fridge about an hour before you're ready to cook it so it comes up to room temperature before you roast it. Give it a good rinse and then pat it dry with paper towels, making sure you soak up any water in the cavity.

2. Season the turkey inside and out with salt and pepper. Drizzle it with a good amount of olive oil, add a few good sprinkles of salt and pepper, and then rub this seasoning all over the bird, making sure you get into all the nooks and crannies.

3. Carefully loosen the skin from the breast, thighs, and legs of the turkey by sliding your fingers between the skin and the meat.

4. Blend together the butter, sage, rosemary, thyme, and pepper.

5. Push the flavored butter between the skin and the meat. Pat the surface of the skin to evenly distribute the butter over the meat.

6. Preheat your oven to 450°F and then get started on your stuffing. Pour 1 to 2 tablespoons of the olive oil into a large pan on medium heat and fry the chopped onion for about 10 minutes or until it softens. Stir in a good pinch of the salt and pepper, nutmeg, and chopped sage leaves. Continue to fry the mixture and stir for an additional 1 to 2 minutes.

7. Spoon the onion mixture into a large bowl and let it cool completely. Once it is cooled, add the ground pork and bread crumbs and use your hands to scrunch everything together. Once it's mixed well, shape the stuffing into a ball, and then cover the bowl and chill it until you're ready to stuff the turkey.

8. Pull back the skin at the neck end of the turkey so you can see a cavity and push about half the stuffing inside the turkey. Then pull and fold the skin over the opening and tuck it under the bird so it looks nice.

9. Turn the turkey around and drop a few small portions of the stuffing into the larger cavity along with the clementine halves and a few sprigs of rosemary.

10. Place some of the roughly chopped vegetables and fruit on the bottom of a roasting pan and place the turkey on top. Surround the turkey with the remaining chopped carrots, orange, apples, celery, potatoes, and rosemary springs.

11. Cover the turkey with foil and then put it in the hot oven and immediately turn the temperature down to 350°F.

12. Cook the turkey for about 15 to 20 minutes per pound. The 10-pound bird in this recipe will take about 2½ to 3 hours and 20 minutes.

13. After 2½ hours, remove the foil so the skin can become golden and crispy.

14. When the turkey is done, carefully lift the turkey out of the roasting pan and rest the turkey on a board covered loosely with foil for at least 1 hour, preferably 2 hours for bigger birds.

15. When the resting time is nearly ended, skim the surface fat from the roasting tray and add the flour and stock. Place the tray on the stove and bring the mixture to a boil on high heat. When the gravy starts to thicken, strain it into a bowl. Enjoy!

Serves: 6 | Prep and Cook Time: 3 hours and 40 minutes to 4 hours and 30 minutes, plus 1 to 2 hours to rest

ROYAL DESSERTS

CHOCOLATE GODDESS CAKE

Priestesses who worship the goddess of harvest and fertility know that one of the best ways to heal the mind, body, and soul is through food like this rich chocolate cake. Whether you're making your way to the temple to ask for spiritual guidance or to recover from a gruesome wound you got when fighting a particularly strong cursed beast, a cake like this will rejuvenate you more than any medicine could.

FOR THE CAKE

coconut oil or butter, for greasing the cake pans

⅔ cup almond flour

⅔ cup cocoa

7 ounces maple syrup

½ cup coconut sugar

3 small eggs

¼ cup ground flaxseed

2¾ tablespoons tapioca starch

2 teaspoons vanilla extract

1 teaspoon salt

FOR THE FROSTING

10 ounces canned coconut cream

1 cup cashews, soaked for 4 to 5 hours

10 pitted soft dates

5 to 6 tablespoons canned coconut milk

4 tablespoons cocoa powder

½ cup dark chocolate, melted

FOR THE CHOCOLATE SAUCE

½ cup canned coconut milk

5 tablespoons cocoa paste or dark chocolate (over 70 percent cocoa)

7 teaspoons coconut oil

pinch of salt

cocoa nibs

1. Preheat the oven to 320°F. Line three 7-inch cake pans with parchment paper. Grease the pans with coconut oil or butter and set aside.

2. To make the cake, in a large bowl, place all ingredients for the cake and mix until they are well combined and smooth. Divide the batter into 3 equal parts and pour into the lined and greased pans. Bake one cake at a time, until a toothpick inserted in the middle of the cake comes out clean, about 30 to 35 minutes each. Allow the cakes to cool completely before removing from the cake pan.

3. To make the frosting, put the coconut cream, cashews, dates, and coconut milk in a food processor. Blend the mixture until it is smooth. Add the remaining ingredients, and blend again.

4. To prepare the sauce, place all the ingredients (except for the cocoa nibs) in a double boiler or water bath and melt them. Stir until the mixture is smooth, then cool it until it reaches a density that allows you to drizzle the sauce on the cake.

5. To assemble the cake, spread the first layer with ⅓ of the frosting. Repeat this step with the remaining layers. Drizzle the cake with the chocolate sauce and sprinkle the cake with cocoa nibs. Place the cake in the refrigerator for 12 hours.

6. When you are ready to serve the cake, cut it with a knife dipped in hot water. Serve the cake with extra chocolate sauce and enjoy!

Serves: 8 | Prep and Cook Time: 2 hours to 2 hours and 5 minutes, plus 12 hours to refrigerate

RESTORING RICE KRISPIES

These rice treats have the perfect balance of sweet and salty, making them the perfect post-dinner snack. After fully recovering from a few physical and mental wounds or just taking a short break from a life of hunting monsters, a certain witcher is sure to leave the temple in better condition than he was when he arrived, and often he'll leave with a few delicious treats for the journey ahead.

cooking spray
3 tablespoons butter, salted or unsalted

1¾ cups marshmallows, chopped
6 cups Rice Krispies

1. Spray a 9 x 13-inch pan with nonstick cooking spray and set it aside. Spray a large pot and a rubber scraper with nonstick cooking spray.

2. Place the pot over medium heat and melt the butter. Add the marshmallows and stir to coat them in butter. Continue stirring until the marshmallows have completely melted. Remove the mixture from the heat.

3. Pour the cereal into the pot and stir to coat it in the melted marshmallow mixture. Pour the mixture into the prepared pan.

4. Using lightly greased fingers, press the mixture down to flatten the top. Cool 15 to 30 minutes before cutting it into squares. Enjoy!

Serves: 6 | Prep and Cook Times: 30 to 45 minutes

DRIED FRUIT

A simple but favorite dessert or snack for the citizens of one of the biggest cities on the Continent. This dessert is enjoyed by both peasants and royalty alike, and one will always find a welcoming bowl of dried fruit in someone's home.

2 apples
2 apricots
4 strawberries

2 bananas
2 oranges
2 handfuls blueberries

1. Wash and dry all the fruits.

2. Core and slice the apples. Slice the apricots in half and remove the pits. Slice the strawberries, bananas, and oranges. Remove the seeds from the oranges.

3. Arrange the fruits on the dehydrator trays and set the heat to 110°F. Berries and apples will be ready first, after 7 to 12 hours. Apricots and bananas will be ready in 12 to 16 hours, and the oranges will be ready last. The time depends on the thickness and the amount of water in the fruit.

4. When the fruits get crispy, they are ready. Store in an airtight container for up to 3 months.

Serves: 4 | Prep and Cook Time: 7 hours and 15 minutes to 16 hours and 15 minutes

HONEY CAKES FOR A COIN

Even hardened masters training the next generation of young witchers have their guilty pleasures. Honey cake as sweet as this one makes one forget the cold, hard days spent training, sword fighting, and learning new magic. And for this master, this dessert brings back memories of a life spent as a young servant boy sharing stolen cakes with his childhood friend.

cooking spray
2 cups all-purpose flour
½ teaspoon salt
½ teaspoon baking soda
½ cup unsalted butter, softened

1 cup honey
3 large eggs
¼ teaspoon almond extract
½ cup sour cream
powdered sugar, for serving

1. Preheat the oven to 350°F. Line a 9-inch round cake pan with parchment and grease it with cooking spray.

2. In a large bowl, whisk together the flour, salt, and baking soda.

3. In another large bowl, use a hand mixer to beat the butter and honey together until the butter is smooth and the mixture is light and creamy.

4. Add the eggs one at a time, beating well after each addition, and then add the almond extract. Add the dry ingredients and beat until they are just barely combined; then add the sour cream and beat the mixture until it is just combined.

5. Pour the batter into the prepared cake pan and bake the cake until a toothpick inserted in the middle comes out clean, about 35 minutes. Let cool.

6. Dust the cake with the powdered sugar and serve.

Serves: 6 | Prep and Cook Time: 55 minutes

HAUNTED HONEYCOMB

A small, sweet snack like this honeycomb is often a favorite of kids in certain countries across the Continent. While children are given honeycomb as a reward for good behavior, a certain white-haired witcher got his share of this treat when he stumbled upon a mischievous godling and found her haunted house full of honeycomb.

1½ cups white sugar
½ cup honey
⅓ cup water

2 tablespoons golden syrup
2 teaspoons baking soda

1. Line a sheet pan with baking paper.

2. In a medium saucepan, combine the sugar, honey, water, and golden syrup. Place the saucepan over low heat and cook, stirring occasionally, for 5 to 7 minutes or until the sugar dissolves. Increase the heat to high and bring the mixture to a boil.

3. Cook, without stirring, for 5 to 7 minutes or until the syrup reaches 309°F on a candy thermometer. Remove the saucepan from the heat and set it aside for the syrup's bubbles to subside.

4. Add the baking soda and quickly stir the mixture with a wooden spoon until the ingredients are combined. The mixture will bubble and foam. Pour it onto the lined sheet pan and set it aside to cool completely.

5. Turn the honeycomb onto a clean surface. Break it into large pieces. Store it in an airtight container at room temperature for 3 to 4 days.

Serves: 4 | Prep and Cook Time: 30 minutes to 35 minutes

TRAIL OF TREATS

Cookies as delicious as these would make anyone brave in even the scariest of places. In search of his destined child, the witcher heads to a dangerous bog where a few old crones tell him that the child he's looking for set off following a trail of sweet treats through the bog.

2¾ cups all-purpose flour
2 teaspoons cornstarch
½ teaspoon baking soda
¼ teaspoon salt
1 cup unsalted butter

1¼ cups plus ⅓ cup white sugar, divided
1 large egg
1 large egg yolk
2 teaspoons vanilla extract
¼ teaspoon almond extract (optional)

1. Preheat the oven to 350°F. Line 2 cookie sheets with parchment paper and set them aside.

2. In a medium bowl, whisk together the flour, cornstarch, baking soda, and salt.

3. In a separate large bowl, beat together the butter and 1¼ cups sugar until fluffy.

4. Beat in the egg, egg yolk, vanilla extract, and almond extract, if using.

5. With the mixer on low speed, beat the flour mixture into the butter mixture about ½ cup at a time. Pour the remaining ⅓ cup sugar onto a plate.

6. Form the dough into balls about the size of 1 tablespoon. Roll each ball in the sugar and place each of them 2 inches apart on the lined cookie sheet.

7. Bake the cookies 1 sheet at a time on the middle rack of the oven for 8 to 10 minutes, or until the tops look just set.

8. Cool the cookies for at least 10 minutes, and then transfer them to a wire rack to cool completely.

Serves: 10 | Prep and Cook Time: 35 to 40 minutes

PINEAPPLE UPSIDE-DOWN CAKE

A magnificent dessert, this Pineapple Upside-Down Cake (and its name in particular) feels especially appropriate to end the banquet held in honor of a princess and her royal family—the last banquet before her city was invaded and the princess's life was turned upside down.

FOR THE PINEAPPLE TOPPING

¾ cup light brown sugar, packed

¼ cup unsalted butter

2 tablespoons pineapple juice, from the canned pineapple

1 (20-ounce) can pineapple rings in juice, drained, reserving juice

13 maraschino cherries

FOR THE CAKE

vegetable cooking spray

2 cups all-purpose flour

½ teaspoon salt

2½ teaspoons baking powder

¼ teaspoon baking soda

¾ cup granulated sugar

2 large eggs

¾ cup buttermilk

¼ cup reserved pineapple juice

½ cup unsalted butter, melted and cooled

1 teaspoon vanilla extract

1. Preheat the oven to 350°F. Lightly spray an 11-inch round cake pan (it must be at least 2 inches deep) with vegetable cooking spray. Set it aside.

2. To make the topping, in a small saucepan, combine the brown sugar, butter, and 2 tablespoons of pineapple juice. Warm the mixture over medium heat until the butter is melted and the sugar is dissolved. Pour the warm sauce into the prepared pan.

3. Place 7 pineapple rings in the pan, starting by centering one in the middle. Add the remaining 6 rings around the center. Place a cherry in the middle of each ring and between them. Set the pan aside while preparing the cake batter.

4. To prepare the cake, in a large mixing bowl, whisk together the flour, salt, baking powder, baking soda, and granulated sugar. Make a well in the center and set the bowl aside.

5. In a small mixing bowl, lightly whisk the eggs. Add the buttermilk, reserved pineapple juice, butter, and vanilla. Whisk the mixture until it is blended.

6. Pour the buttermilk mixture into the flour mixture and gently fold them together with a spatula until the flour is incorporated. The batter will be thick and lumpy. Gently scoop dollops of the batter into the prepared pan, taking care not to move the pineapple rings. Gently smooth the top.

7. Place the cake pan on a foil-lined baking sheet and bake it at 350°F until a toothpick comes out with no wet batter, about 45 to 50 minutes. Tent the cake with foil if it overbrowns. Take it out of the oven and allow the cake to cool in the pan for 15 to 20 minutes.

8. Invert a serving platter over the cake pan. Invert the cake pan and platter together, and then lift off the cake pan. Cool the cake to room temperature, slice, and serve.

Serves: 8 | Prep and Cook Time: 1 hour and 25 minutes to 1 hour and 35 minutes

HONEY-AND-SPICE CAKE

The central region of the Continent is home to some of the most delectable wine and treats, and its Honey-and-Spice Cake is a favorite across the land. When made by a certain famous chef, this recipe is not just a dessert—it's art.

1½ cups honey, divided

¼ cup water

1 cup, plus 2 tablespoons sugar

14 tablespoons unsalted butter, cut into ½-inch pieces

6 large eggs

2½ teaspoons baking soda

1¼ teaspoons fine sea salt, divided

1 teaspoon ground cinnamon

1 teaspoon ginger powder

¼ teaspoon ground nutmeg

3¾ cups all-purpose flour

1¼ cups dulce de leche

4¾ cups cream cheese, chilled and divided

1. Preheat the oven to 375°F. Take 12 baking-sheet-size pieces of parchment paper and on each one, trace circles around a 9-inch pie or cake pan. Set aside.

2. Make a water bath: Fill a small saucepan with 1 inch of water, and set the saucepan over medium heat.

3. Place ¾ cup of honey in a 2-quart saucepan and set it over high heat. Bring the honey to a simmer, and then reduce the heat to medium. After about 3 minutes, the honey will begin to foam intensely. Stir the honey occasionally with a wooden spoon, keeping a close eye on the honey. Cook the honey until it begins to smoke, and then turn off the heat and carefully add the ¼ cup water. Allow the burnt honey to sputter until it stops bubbling. Whisk to combine the water and burnt honey, then pour the mixture into a heatproof measuring cup with a spout.

Place the cup in the prepared water bath to keep the burnt honey liquid.

4. Fill a medium saucepan with 2 inches of water, and bring it to a simmer. Combine ¼ cup of the burnt honey, ¾ cup of the honey, sugar, and butter in a large metal mixing bowl, and place the bowl over the pan of water.

5. Crack the eggs into a small bowl and set the bowl aside. Stir together the baking soda, ¾ teaspoon sea salt, cinnamon, ginger, and nutmeg in a separate small bowl.

6. When the butter has melted, whisk the honey mixture to combine it in thoroughly. Use your finger to test the temperature of the mixture. When it's warm, add the eggs while whisking. When the mixture returns to the same temperature, add the cinnamon mixture and continue whisking for an additional 30 seconds. The batter will begin to foam. Remove the bowl from the water bath, and allow it to cool until it's warm.

7. Place the flour in a fine-mesh sieve, and sift it over the batter in 3 batches, whisking to incorporate the flour completely with each addition. The batter should be completely smooth. The batter will spread more easily when it's warm, so pour half of it into a small bowl and cover it with plastic wrap. Place the bowl in a warm spot.

8. Place one of the circle cut outs of parchment, tracing side down, on a baking sheet, and spoon onto the parchment a heaping ⅓ cup of batter. Use an offset spatula to evenly spread the batter to the edges of the circle. It will seem like just barely enough batter; do your best to get the layer even and perfectly circular. Repeat this step with the remaining circles of parchment until you're out of baking sheets to hold the circles of batter. (You may have to bake a few batter circles first if you do not have enough baking sheets to hold all 12 batter circles at one time.) Then continue this process the with remaining half of batter and parchment circles. You will end up with 12 circles of batter.

9. Bake as many layers at a time as possible, for 6 to 7 minutes, until the cake batter turns a deep caramel color and springs back to the touch. For the first round, set the timer for 4 minutes to rotate pans if needed to ensure even cooking. Check the cakes again at 6 minutes. Do not overbake.

10. When each layer is done, slide the parchment off the pan to prevent overbaking. If reusing baking sheets to cook remaining layers while they are still hot, reduce the cooking time to 5 to 6 minutes.

11. When all the cake layers are cool enough to handle, examine them. If any spread outside the traced circles as they baked, use a sharp knife or pair of scissors to trim them. Before the cakes cool entirely, pull each one carefully from the parchment, then place each one back on the parchment on a flat surface and allow them to cool completely.

12. When all the layers are baked, reduce the oven temperature to 250°F and allow the cake layers to cool for 30 minutes. Return the least attractive layer to a baking sheet and place it in the oven to toast until it is deep reddish brown and dry, about 15 minutes. Allow it to cool, and then use a food processor to grind it into fine crumbs. Cover and set aside the crumbs.

13. Place the remaining ½ cup of the burned honey, dulce de leche, and ½ teaspoon fine sea salt into a medium bowl. Whisk by hand until combined, then slowly pour in ¾ cup cream cheese and mix until the mixture is homogeneous. Chill the mixture until it cools completely, about 30 minutes.

14. Pour 4 cups of the cream cheese into the bowl of a stand mixer, and attach the whisk attachment. Whip the cheese at medium speed until it forms soft peaks, and then add the honey mixture and whip the frosting until it forms medium stiff peaks.

15. Assemble the cake on a 10-inch cardboard circle or flat serving plate. Place a cake layer in the center of the cardboard, and then spoon a heaping cup of frosting onto the center. Use an offset spatula to spread the frosting evenly, leaving a ¼-inch ring unfrosted around the edge. Place the next layer atop the frosting, center it, and repeat the frosting process. Don't be afraid to manhandle the cake to align the layers as you continue stacking. If necessary, make up for any doming in the center by spreading more frosting to the outer edges of each layer.

16. After you assemble the last layer, spread another scant cup of frosting over the top. Use any leftover frosting to smooth out the sides of the cake. Sprinkle the top and sides with cake crumbs.

17. Chill overnight. Serve chilled. Enjoy!

Serves: 6 | Prep and Cook Time: 2 hours to 2 hours and 15 minutes, plus overnight to chill

CONVERSIONS

VOLUME

US	US Equivalent	Metric
1 tablespoon (3 teaspoons)	½ fluid ounce	15 milliliters
¼ cup	2 fluid ounces	60 milliliters
⅓ cup	3 fluid ounces	90 milliliters
½ cup	4 fluid ounces	120 milliliters
⅔ cup	5 fluid ounces	150 milliliters
¾ cup	6 fluid ounces	180 milliliters
1 cup	8 fluid ounces	240 milliliters
2 cups	16 fluid ounces	480 milliliters

WEIGHT

US	Metric
½ ounce	15 grams
1 ounce	30 grams
2 ounces	60 grams
¼ pound	115 grams
⅓ pound	150 grams
½ pound	225 grams
¾ pound	350 grams
1 pound	450 grams

TEMPERATURE

Fahrenheit (°F)	Celsius (°C)	Fahrenheit (°F)	Celsius (°C)
70°F	20°C	220°F	105°C
100°F	40°C	240°F	115°C
120°F	50°C	260°F	125°C
130°F	55°C	280°F	140°C
140°F	60°C	300°F	150°C
150°F	65°C	325°F	165°C
160°F	70°C	350°F	175°C
170°F	75°C	375°F	190°C
180°F	80°C	400°F	200°C
190°F	90°C	425°F	220°C
200°F	95°C	450°F	230°C

RECIPE INDEX

ABOUT THE CONTRIBUTORS

Local New Orleanian and author **Trey Guillory** has loved stories his entire life. From following the adventuring hobbits in *Lord of the Rings*, rooting for the defense of Earth from aliens in *Ender's Game*, and solving mysteries with Sherlock Holmes, no story or genre was too big for him to tackle.

Now a writer himself, he strives to create and contribute the same type of literature that has inspired him his entire life. A self-proclaimed professional geek, he holds a master's degree in English and journalism from the University of New Orleans. He now spends his time fanboying and attending conventions across the Gulf Coast in order to meet others and share his passions for these fandoms and stories.

Nevyana Dimitrova is a 27-year-old professional food photographer and recipe developer who has loved cooking since she was a little girl. She tells stories through the food she prepares and captures in her photos. The magic of nature inspires her constantly, and she always works with absolute passion on her culinary creations.